University
of Worcester

informa

D1644467

The ancient
Egyptians

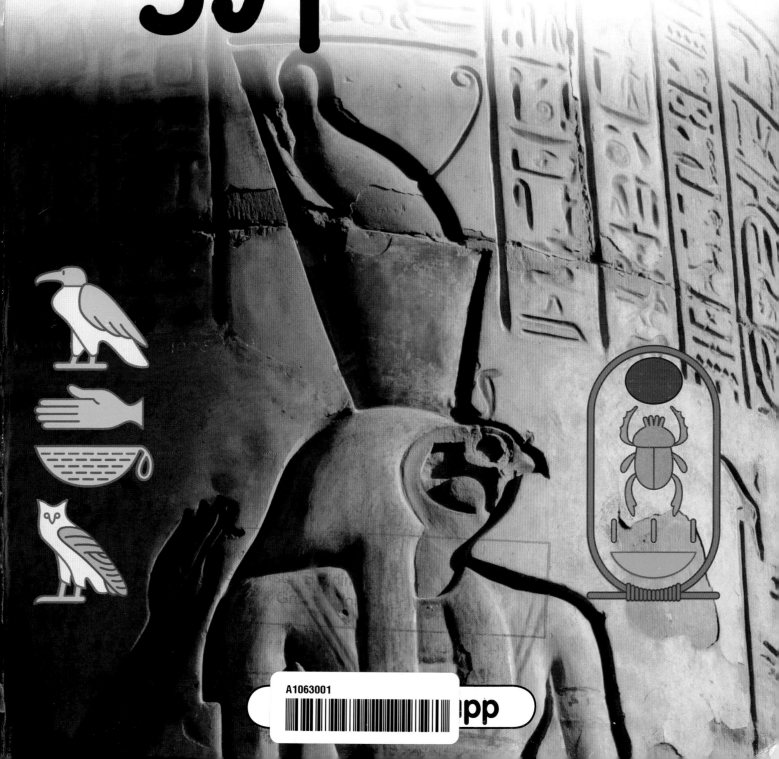

pp

◀ Obelisk with hieroglyphs.

Curriculum Visions

Curriculum Visions is a registered trademark of Atlantic Europe Publishing Company Ltd.

There's more on-line

There's more about other great Curriculum Visions packs and a wealth of supporting information available at our dedicated web site. Visit:

www.CurriculumVisions.com

✦ Atlantic Europe Publishing

First published in 2006 by
Atlantic Europe Publishing Company Ltd.
Copyright © 2006
Atlantic Europe Publishing Company Ltd.

Author
Brian Knapp, BSc, PhD

Art Director
Duncan McCrae, BSc

Senior Designer
Adele Humphries, BA, PGCE

Editor
Robert Anderson, BA, PGCE, and Lisa Magloff, MA

Designed and produced by
EARTHSCAPE EDITIONS

Printed in China by
WKT Company Ltd

The ancient Egyptians – *Curriculum Visions*
A CIP record for this book is available from the British Library

Paperback ISBN-10: 1 86214 450 8 (**ISBN-13**: 978 1 86214 450 7)
Hardback ISBN-10: 1 86214 452 4 (**ISBN-13**: 978 1 86214 452 1)

Illustrations
David Woodroffe

Picture credits
All photographs are from the Earthscape Editions photolibrary except the following:
Bridgeman Art Archive page 17 (Tutankhamun throne); *bygonetimes/Alamy* page 16–17 (Tutankhamun coffin); *Freestock.com* pages 11 (Tutankhamun coffin), 19 (woman grinding corn), 34 (stone sarcophagus), 45 (Akhenaten); *The Granger Collection, New York* pages 6 and 15 (Tutankhamun mask), 7 (mummy), 14 (grave goods), 23 (Rosetta Stone); 33 (mummy), 34 (Tutankhamun tomb), 35 (coffins).

This product is manufactured from sustainable managed forests. For every tree cut down at least one more is planted.

⚠ Look after our world heritage!

It is easy to talk about looking after our heritage, but we each have to help. Help is often small things, like being careful when you walk around old buildings, and not leaving scratch marks on anything that you visit. It doesn't take a lot of effort – just attitude.

Contents

Visiting ancient Egypt

Many people visit ancient Egypt each year. It is particularly easy to visit because nearly all of the remains are next to the Nile. Many people explore this ancient civilisation by travelling on a Nile boat, a kind of floating hotel and learning from the wisdom of an experienced Egyptologist.

▶ **A colossal seated statue.**

Who were the ancient Egyptians?

The ancient Egyptians were one of the world's great civilisations.

The ancient Egyptians were one of the world's first great **CIVILISATIONS**, whose skills in crafts were equal to anything we can do today (picture ①).

The ancient Egyptian civilisation lasted longer than the whole of the Christian era. Yet they lived in one of the places which you might think was the least promising – they lived in the desert of North East Africa.

What brought them all together in such a remarkable way was one of the world's great rivers – the Nile – which runs like an arrow through the heart of the desert. It gave food, water and a means of getting about. It was the lifeblood of the ancient Egyptian empire. But it was also seen as a prize by people living nearby, and because of this the Egyptians became battle hardened warriors.

▼ ① **The ancient Egyptians told us much about themselves through carvings on temples, such as this one at Philae, near modern Aswan.**

▼ ② You are looking straight into the eyes of PHARAOH Tutankhamun of ancient Egypt. This head was carved about 3,000 years ago in a region known as UPPER EGYPT. It is not a true likeness, but carved in a particular style that ancient Egyptians thought pleasing.

Egypt is a desert land where the Sun always shines and the night sky is filled with twinkling lights. The Egyptians believed the sky and their land were connected, the heavens being the home of the gods and where people might go when they died.

Because their only source of water was the River Nile, this, together with the Sun and the night sky, controlled everything they did (picture ③).

The ancient Egyptians produced spectacular temples and **PYRAMIDS** of amazing size. But now their civilisation has vanished. So how do we know about them? Finding out about these people, from what they have left behind, makes the story of this book (picture ②).

▼ ③ The pyramid of Khafre at Giza seen silhouetted against the Sun. The pyramids were built in worship of the Sun god (see page 28).

What is famous about the ancient Egyptians?

Ancient Egypt is famous for pyramids, mummies and the fabulous riches of king Tutankhamun.

Here are some things that you may think the ancient Egyptians are famous for, and some of the questions about ancient Egypt that they raise.

▲ One of the most famous objects made by the ancient Egyptians is the golden mask of Tutankhamun. But why was it made, and who was Tutankhamun?

▲ We have all seen pictures of the Sphinx, but what is it and who was it built for?

▲ Ancient Egyptians are famous for their picture writing (HIEROGLYPHICS). These hieroglyphs stand for Tutankhamun. How do we know?

▶ Most people have heard of mummies, but what were they, and is this one?

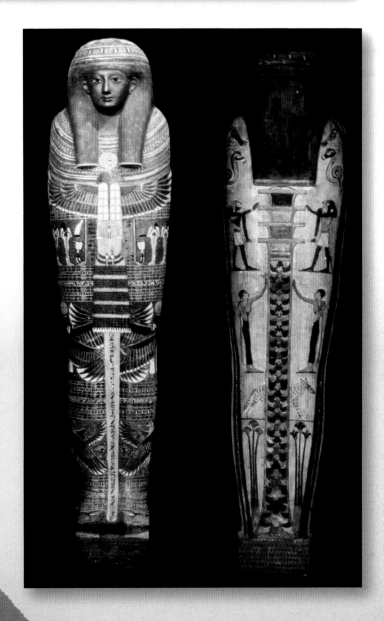

Famous things like **MUMMIES**, pyramids and the riches of Tutankhamun are all part of ancient Egypt, but from them alone you cannot get a very true picture of ancient Egyptian times. The purpose of this book is to set these things into a history of what happened and to explain why the ancient Egyptians lived and believed the way they did. It is a fascinating story.

◀▶ More than anything else we probably know the ancient Egyptians from the pyramids. But what were they for?

Where was ancient Egypt?

If we make a map of all of the places where ancient Egyptian remains can be found, we see an extraordinarily long land, shaped like a flower on a long stalk.

The ancient Egyptians were united because they all lived along – and depended on – the River Nile.

The River Nile made it possible for people in ancient Egypt to grow food in the desert, and to transport food, people and building materials long distances. Without the river only a very few people could have lived in Egypt.

The yearly ebb and flow of the river's waters also set the pace of life for the ancient Egyptians.

How do you know that nearly all the ancient Egyptians lived close to the river? **ARCHAEOLOGISTS** have plotted the remains of ancient Egypt on a map (picture ①). On these pages you can also see some of the best known of these remains.

▲ Pyramids and the Sphinx, Giza.

▼ Valley of the Kings (where Tutankhamun was buried), Luxor.

▼ Temple of Philae, near modern Aswan.

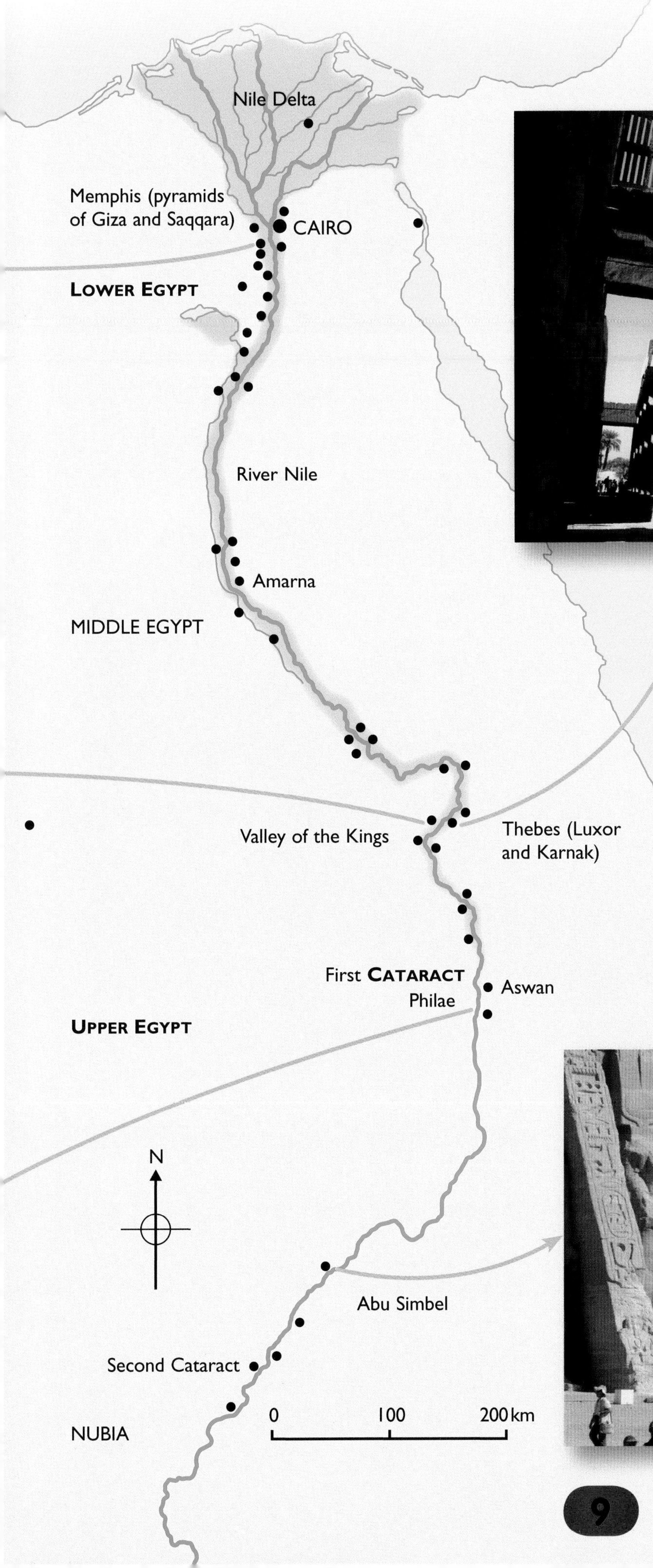

Megiddo battle

Kadesh battle

Nile Delta

Memphis (pyramids
of Giza and Saqqara)

CAIRO

LOWER EGYPT

River Nile

Amarna

MIDDLE EGYPT

Valley of the Kings

Thebes (Luxor
and Karnak)

First **CATARACT**

Philae

Aswan

UPPER EGYPT

N

Abu Simbel

Second Cataract

NUBIA

0   100   200 km

▲ Temples at Thebes.

◀ ① Here you can see why
everyone stayed close to the
Nile. The green is fertile
farmland, the yellow is desert.
The Nile allowed farmers to
grow crops.

● Dots show important ancient Egyptian sites.

▼ Temple of Abu Simbel.

How long did the ancient Egyptian kingdom last?

The ancient Egyptian kingdom lasted for more than 3,000 years and included about 30 dynasties of kings.

The ancient Egyptian civilisation can be traced back to 5000 BC. However, they first began to keep records from about 3000 BC and it is from this time that we get to know about kings, their names and what they did.

This long period of recorded time is divided up into three main periods (picture ①): the Old Kingdom (the days of the **PYRAMIDS**), the Middle Kingdom and the New Kingdom (the days of king Tutankhamun).

▼ ① Ancient Egyptian times.

2800 BC
First capital at Memphis (near modern Cairo). First ever pyramid – the Step Pyramid.

2500 BC
The Great Pyramids are built at Giza near modern Cairo.

5000 BC
The earliest traces of the ancient Egyptian civilisation.

3000 BC
Earliest known Egyptian letter writing (hieroglyphics). First kings of Egypt.

5000 BC	4000 BC	3000 BC	2000 BC

YEARS AGO

Earliest Egypt

1st to 2nd dynasties	2650–1975 BC Old Kingdom	1975–1539 BC Middle Kingdom

Each of these periods are themselves divided into times ruled by related kings, known as **DYNASTIES** (just as English history is divided into periods named after families of kings, such as the Tudors).

Kings became known as **PHARAOHS**, and this is the term we shall use, although it was not the official title they used themselves.

When a king's line was lost because he had no heirs, a new dynasty started.

After the New Kingdom, Egypt had no more strong rulers and it was conquered several times. In 332 BC it was conquered by the Greeks and it later became a part of the Roman empire.

Abu Simbel

Time of temple building at Thebes (Luxor and Karnak).

332–375 AD
Greek and Roman period.
Egypt conquered by Alexander the Great. Alexander's general Ptolemy becomes pharaoh. Rosetta Stone carved. Cleopatra rules Egypt. Egypt becomes a province of the Roman empire and stops being an independent country.

Tutankhamun's tomb

1000 BC	0	1000 AD	2000 AD

1539–1075 BC
New Kingdom

1075–332 BC
Late Period
Egypt conquered several times but remains an independent country.

Weblink: www.CurriculumVisions.com

Egypt, land of the Nile

The Nile was vital to the ancient Egyptians, just as it is to Egyptians today. So we can use modern pictures to help us imagine what the land of ancient Egypt was like.

▼ ① This ancient Egyptian tomb picture shows a farmer with a whip encouraging his oxen to plough the soil.

For most of its length the Nile valley is just a narrow strip of land a few kilometres wide. Only in the north does the land open out into the fan shape of the Nile **DELTA** and thus provide extra land for farming (see map on page 9).

Farmers ancient and modern

How do we know how people used the Nile and its lands in ancient times? Fortunately, ancient Egyptian people drew their world on the walls and roofs of their tombs.

In picture ① you can clearly see a farmer working the land, the tools he

▲ ② Boats were a vital part of life on Earth and life in the heavens, as shown by this tomb painting. It shows many people being taken by boat into the afterlife, accompanied by the god Horus (the falcon) and the god Osiris (the bird with a plumed crown).

◀ ③ A grove of date palm trees with clusters of brown dates hanging from them.

▼ ④ A farmer walking behind his plough with his son sowing seed just as he might have done 4,000 years ago.

◀ ⑤ This modern picture shows the area of farmland beside the Nile. The boat is a felucca, invented after the time of the ancient Egyptians who mostly used boats with oars as they had no shortage of slaves. There is fertile farmland beside the river, but the mountainous desert behind makes it impossible for farmers to spread out far from the Nile.

Boats on the Nile

The Nile was, and still is, important as a way of getting about. We see this in modern Egypt and we can see it in the paintings of the ancient world, too (pictures ② and ⑤).

The Nile provided a link between all of the places of the ancient kingdom (see the map on page 9).

used, the animals he reared and some of the crops he harvested. Much of this traditional life can still be seen today (pictures ③ and ④).

Kingly objects from the past

Because the ancient Egyptians lived a long time ago, most of what they made and used has perished. But what remains gives important clues to what life was like.

There is a desert valley near Luxor in **UPPER EGYPT** where the pharaohs of the New Kingdom were buried. It is called the Valley of the Kings. Here, below a cliff that looks like a natural pyramid, many caves were dug and turned into tombs.

This is where we find the richest source of objects from the time of the ancient Egyptians. Let's look at some of these objects and see what we make of them, and what they can tell us.

The tomb of Tutankhamun

The tomb of the boy pharaoh Tutankhamun is small. For thousands of years it remained undisturbed while the bigger tombs around were ransacked by grave robbers. It was sealed in 1325 BC and from then until 1922, some 3,200 years, no living soul entered the sealed chamber, no light reached it and no dust settled on the objects inside.

▲ ① This is a photograph taken in 1922 showing one of the rooms packed high with GRAVE GOODS. They are things the priests believed the pharaoh would need in the afterlife. The largest object you can see is one side of a bed with supports carved in the shape of a leopard.

This is why, when the archaeologist Howard Carter opened the tomb, he found 32,000 untouched objects inside (picture ①).

Death mask

We know this is a death mask of the pharaoh because it was found on his **MUMMIFIED** body (picture ②). It is made of 11 kg of gold set with semi-precious stones. It tells us that at this time ancient Egypt was a very rich country because it could spare so much gold. It is evidence that the people thought very highly of their pharaoh. It also shows us that the ancient Egyptians were fine craftspeople and that they were very artistic. It also gives clues to the way the pharaoh dressed.

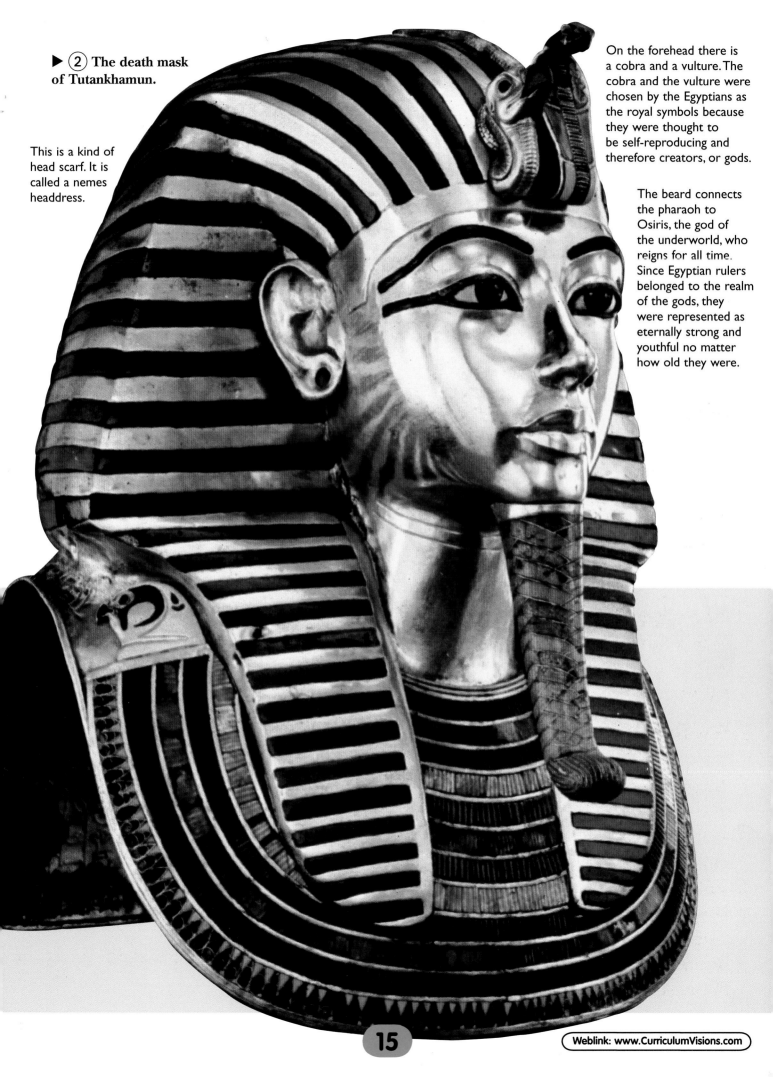

▶ ② **The death mask of Tutankhamun.**

This is a kind of head scarf. It is called a nemes headdress.

On the forehead there is a cobra and a vulture. The cobra and the vulture were chosen by the Egyptians as the royal symbols because they were thought to be self-reproducing and therefore creators, or gods.

The beard connects the pharaoh to Osiris, the god of the underworld, who reigns for all time. Since Egyptian rulers belonged to the realm of the gods, they were represented as eternally strong and youthful no matter how old they were.

15

Tutankhamun's throne

The golden throne (picture ③) has a picture of Tutankhamun and his wife on the back. They are shown with a Sun disc with sunbeams. This is a symbol of the Sun god, Re (or Ra).

The coffin

The body was buried in a stone coffin, or **SARCOPHAGUS**, and in this were three coffins. The innermost coffin was made from 110 kg of gold (picture ④). Like the death mask, it has strips of the rare and beautiful blue stone lapis lazuli set into the gold.

What we can tell from these objects

If we had found no other objects or writings about pharaohs, beyond those you can see here, what could we tell from just this one tomb?

We would know that it was a highly skilled civilisation, that it was wealthy, and that its people thought that it was important to preserve the body after the king died.

We can imagine that the people thought that the pharaoh was some kind of link to the gods that the people believed in.

▶ ③ The throne of Tutankhamun shows the pharaoh and his wife. The Sun god Re stretches out rays of light to the pharaoh. The arms of the throne are made in the shape of lions, protectors of the pharaoh.

◀ ④ This is the inner gold coffin found in Tutankhamun's tomb.

The lives of ordinary people

The homes of ordinary people have rarely survived because they were usually made of mud. But near the Valley of the Kings they were made of stone.

There is a unique valley near to the Valley of the Kings at Thebes (modern Luxor). It is the village in which the people who made the royal burial chambers lived.

▼ ① **This is the village of the workers (Deir el-Medina). This must have been a busy place, with wives cooking food and cleaning clothes while husbands worked at making the royal tombs.**

Picture ① shows a main street with dozens of small stone-built houses on either side. Each house had several rooms.

The upper parts of the houses have disappeared, probably because they were made from mud bricks and so have worn away. The houses may also have had roofs of palm-fronds supported on poles laid across the walls.

Clues to the simple life

A few objects remain that tell us what ordinary people did. Picture ②, for example, shows a woman grinding corn. This small stone object was made at the same time as the Great Pyramids were being built. She has a headdress (called a nemes headcloth) of the same kind as the pharaoh. So we can conclude that this was a traditional style of dress for everyone, not just pharaohs, although we can imagine that the materials used to make the pharaoh's headdress would be finer than for ordinary people.

We can also see just how people ground corn, using a rod-shaped stone rubbed on a flat stone. Looking at this carving allows us to imagine that this was both hard work and hard on the knees.

Pieces of ordinary pottery give us more clues to the ancient Egyptian way of life. For example, picture ④ is a hollowed stone used to make flour. You may care to try to work out what picture ③ is part of. It is made of a simple clay pottery.

▼ ② A statue of a woman grinding corn.

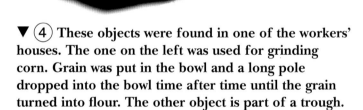

▼ ③ Archaeologists often find just fragments of pottery, like this one, photographed in one of the workers' houses. What do you think it was part of? Clue: imagine the curve continued around.

▼ ④ These objects were found in one of the workers' houses. The one on the left was used for grinding corn. Grain was put in the bowl and a long pole dropped into the bowl time after time until the grain turned into flour. The other object is part of a trough.

Stories in pictures

Some of the most important clues to how the ancient Egyptians lived come from their wall carvings and the writing they made on PAPYRUS.

▶ ② This carving tells us that it was common to use chariots in battle.

▼ ① Ramesses II defeating the neighbouring tribes (the Hittites) at the battle of Kadesh (modern Syria).

Look at some of the pictures of buildings in this book (for example, on pages 4 and 9). You will notice how many of these carvings record events from history (pictures ① and ②).

Clearly, if the ancient Egyptians went to so much trouble, the pictures must have been very important. So what story can they tell us?

Picture ①, for instance, shows the battle of Kadesh (1274 BC) in which the pharaoh Ramesses II (on the left) defeated the neighbouring **HITTITE** people.

Ramesses is drawn large to tell everyone that he won the battle. Below his left hand you can see the Hittite warriors. They are small because they have been defeated.

The carving tells everyone that Egypt was successful in defeating other peoples and that the Egyptians could defend their land. The other large figure is the god Amun. It tells us that Ramesses believed it was Amun's power that helped him to win the battle.

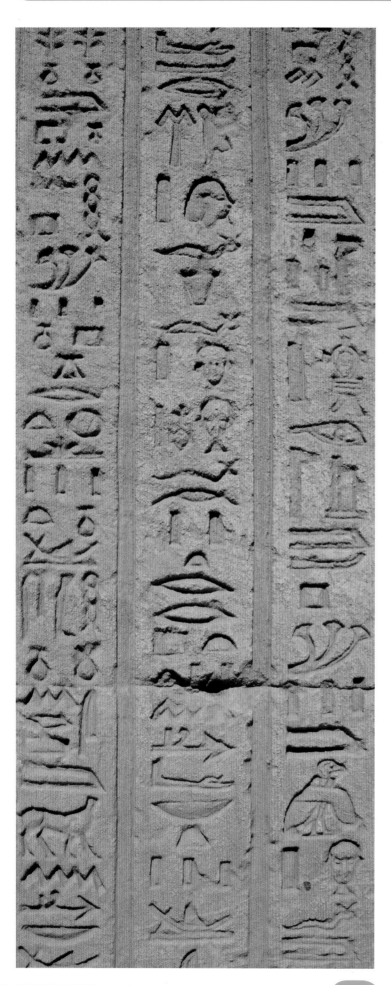

Stories in words – hieroglyphics

Ancient Egyptians also left writing as a record of their lives.

There are many ways to write words. We are used to using the letters of our alphabet. But there are other ways of writing, too. The ancient Egyptians used little pictures based on animals, humans, gods and the tools they used in their work. We call these pictures **HIEROGLYPHS** (a word which comes from the Greek meaning sacred carvings, because they were usually carved in stone) (pictures ① and ②).

Word pictures

Each hieroglyph represents a sound, a letter of the alphabet or even a whole word. Hundreds of pictures are needed for this kind of writing.

The Egyptians used hieroglyphic writing for nearly 3,500 years, beginning in about 3300 BC and lasting into Roman times.

◀ ① **Part of a wall containing hieroglyphs.**

Weblink: www.CurriculumVisions.com

The Rosetta Stone

It is doubtful if we would know what any of the hieroglyphs meant if it weren't for a famous 2 m high tombstone called the Rosetta Stone.

The Rosetta Stone is a tablet written in three different ancient languages: Egyptian (hieroglyphics), Arabic and Greek. This tablet was used to work out the meaning of the hieroglyphs.

▼ The Rosetta Stone – part of a tombstone (stela) from ancient Egypt.

How do you read hieroglyphics?

When we read English, we read from left to right in a straight line. Hieroglyphs were often written in rows or columns and can be read from left to right, right to left, or top to bottom. Sometimes the symbols are placed to make a nice pattern (as in cartouches, pages 24–25).

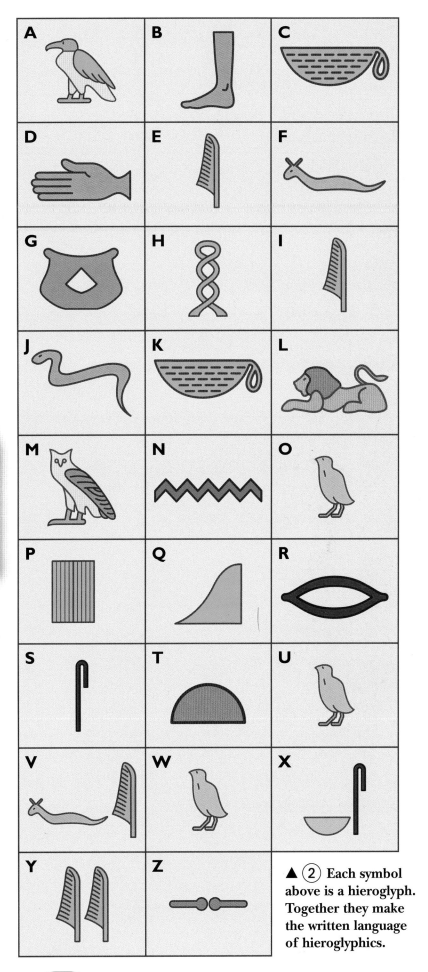

▲ ② Each symbol above is a hieroglyph. Together they make the written language of hieroglyphics.

23

The way to read hieroglyphics (the writing that uses hieroglyphs) is to look at the animals or humans. These always face the direction the line should be read from. For instance, if all the animals are facing right, it should be read from right to left. If all the animals are facing left, it should be read from left to right.

Legal documents were written in rows. Columns were also used on doorways, tomb walls and monuments.

▼▶ ③ Here are the cartouches of some of the important pharaohs. Note that the symbols can be arranged in any order, as shown by the pictures on this page. Each cartouche is the royal name, except for Horemheb and Ramesses, where both birth and royal names are shown.

Khufu

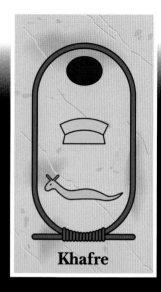

Khafre

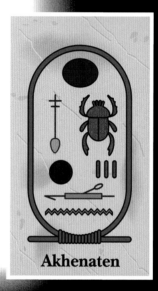

Akhenaten

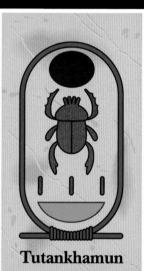

Tutankhamun

Horemheb

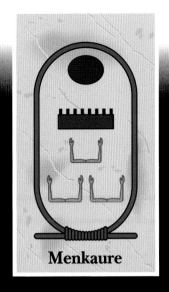

Menkaure

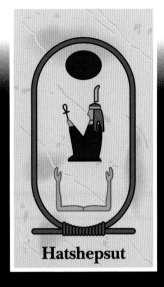

Hatshepsut

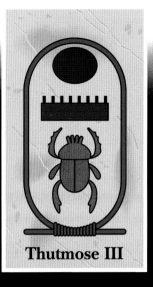

Thutmose III

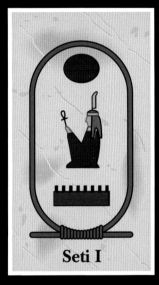

Seti I

Ramesses II

Royal names and cartouches

Like every Egyptian, a future pharaoh was given a name at birth. But on his coronation he was given a royal name as well.

Sometimes groups of hieroglyphs were placed inside an oval ring with a straight line on one side. This is known as a CARTOUCHE (picture ③).

Using a cartouche meant that the name inside was that of a pharaoh.

The ancient Egyptians believed that the cartouche protected the royal name.

The end of hieroglyphics

Because hieroglyphics were so complicated, few people could read them. Over the centuries, ordinary people, and even priests, began to use simpler forms of writing using alphabets. As a result, the hieroglyphic system finally died out.

Pharaohs

The ancient Egyptians believed that the pharaohs were the representatives of the gods on Earth.

Many people use the word pharaoh when talking about the kings of ancient Egypt. But 'pharaoh' originally meant the royal palace where the king lived. However, gradually the term became used for the king himself. Nevertheless, 'pharaoh' never became part of the official title of the king. The pharaoh's official titles were: 'Lord of the Two Lands' and 'High Priest of Every Temple'.

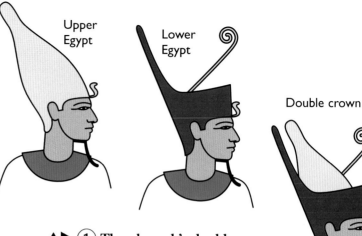

Upper Egypt

Lower Egypt

Double crown

▲▶ ① The pharaoh's double crown is a symbol of the joining of the kingdoms of Upper Egypt (left) and Lower Egypt (centre). See if you can spot the double crown in any of the pictures in this book.

▼ ② Here the pharaoh is kneeling in front of three gods. The pharaoh and the gods are each identified by their headdresses. The main god, Amun-Re, has a double-plumed headdress and he sits at the front. The pharaoh wears the double crown of the united Egypt.

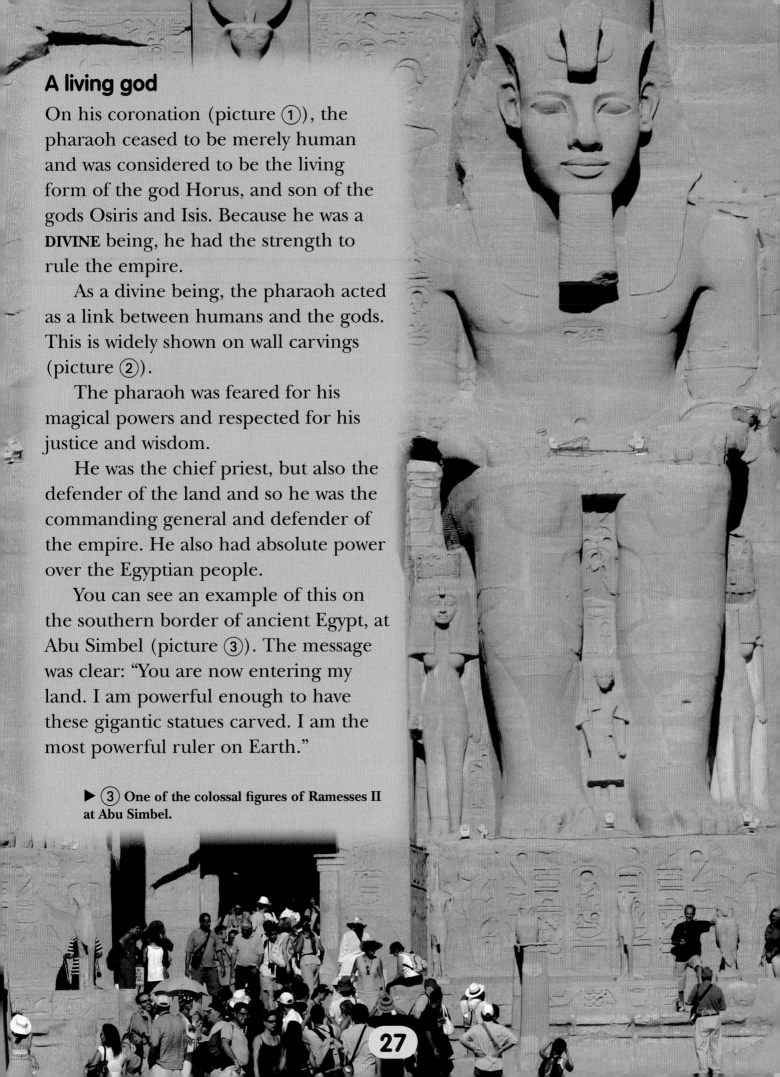

A living god

On his coronation (picture ①), the pharaoh ceased to be merely human and was considered to be the living form of the god Horus, and son of the gods Osiris and Isis. Because he was a **DIVINE** being, he had the strength to rule the empire.

As a divine being, the pharaoh acted as a link between humans and the gods. This is widely shown on wall carvings (picture ②).

The pharaoh was feared for his magical powers and respected for his justice and wisdom.

He was the chief priest, but also the defender of the land and so he was the commanding general and defender of the empire. He also had absolute power over the Egyptian people.

You can see an example of this on the southern border of ancient Egypt, at Abu Simbel (picture ③). The message was clear: "You are now entering my land. I am powerful enough to have these gigantic statues carved. I am the most powerful ruler on Earth."

▶ ③ One of the colossal figures of Ramesses II at Abu Simbel.

Gods of the ancient Egyptians

Everything the ancient Egyptians did was connected to the gods and to the afterlife they believed in.

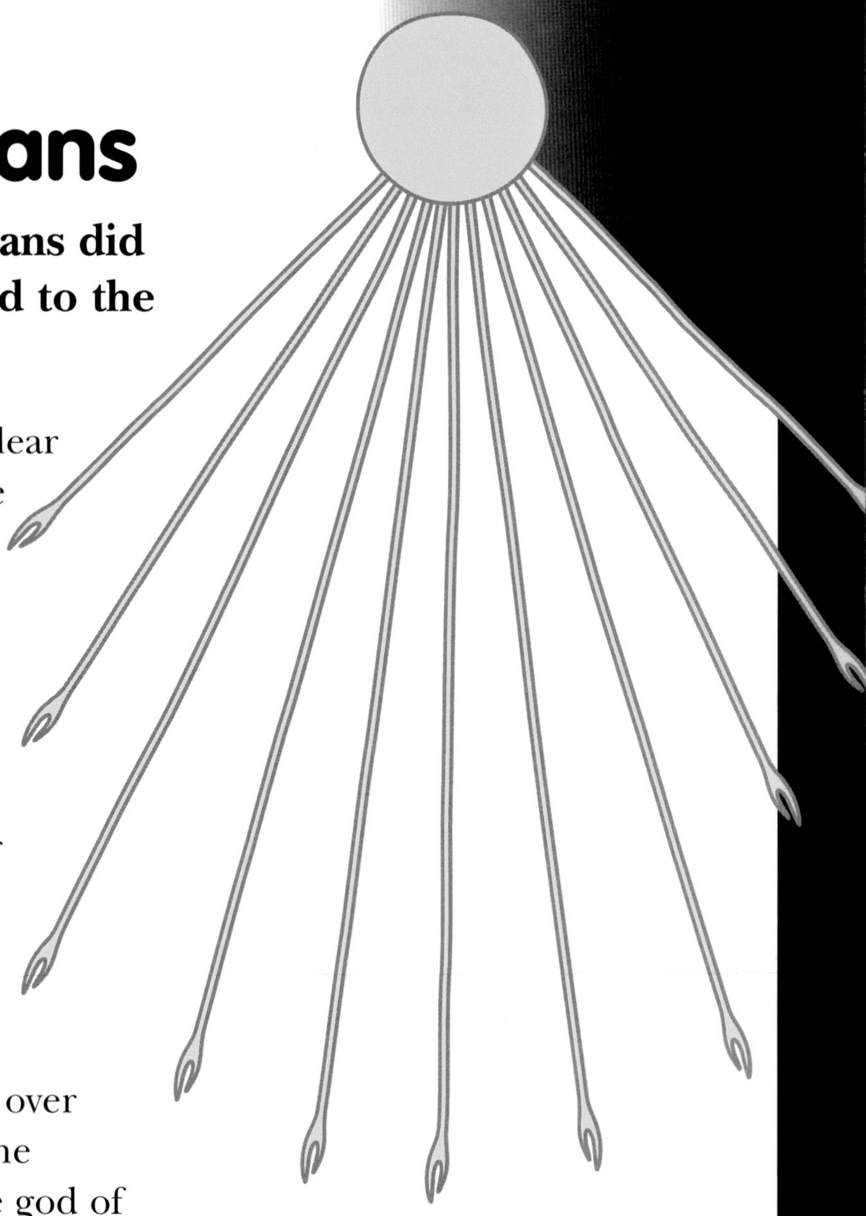

The ancient Egyptians had a very clear view of life and death. They saw the Sun rising each day and giving light. This, they thought, must be a god bringing life to the world.

They saw Egypt as Heaven on Earth (as a promised land). So the Earth was a mirror of heaven, and Egypt was reflected in the stars. For example, they saw the stars of the Milky Way in the night sky as the heavenly version of the River Nile.

They imagined that each important aspect of life was looked over by a particular god. For example, the goddess of the sky was Nut, and the god of the Earth was Geb. Horus was the god that looked after the pharaoh.

The ancient Egyptians thought of most of their gods as connected with animals. For example, the god Thoth was shown with the head of an ibis (a bird, see page 31) and the god Horus as a falcon (see picture opposite).

The gods

The most ancient god was the Sun god, Re (also called Ra and Aten). The early kings even built their pyramids to worship Re.

Re (Ra)

Re (or Ra) was the Egyptian Sun god who created the world and all of the other gods. Every day Re, as the Sun, is recreated and moves across the sky in his SOLAR BOAT. At sunset he plunges into the underworld.

Because of this, kings built pyramids in line with the rising and setting Sun. The gods Horus and Re are often shown as a winged Sun disk.

Re was also connected to the pharaoh, because while Re ruled the Universe, the pharaoh ruled the Earth.

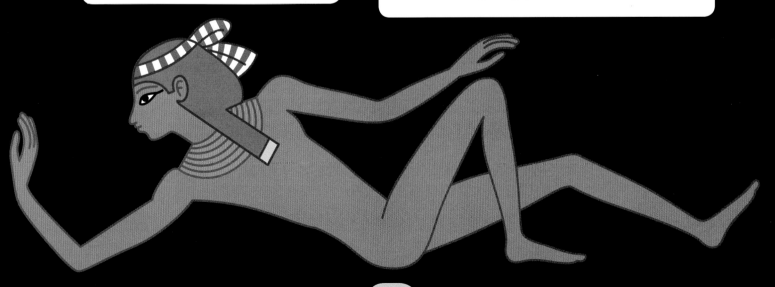

Nut

Nut is the goddess of the sky. She is shown as a naked woman painted with stars, arching over the world, her hands and feet touching the four points of the compass. She is often shown being held up by Shu, the god of the air, and standing over her husband–brother Geb.

Nut is the mother of Osiris and Isis. Nut protects the world from the darkness and its demons. The Sun god Re appears near her feet in the morning, travels along her body during the day, and enters the underworld again at night near her fingers.

Horus

Horus is the prince of gods, who protected and guided the living pharaoh.

He was thought of as the son of Osiris and Isis. In the myth of Horus, he was conceived magically after the death of Osiris, and Isis hid him away on an island to protect him from the wicked god Set. Eventually he kills Set in revenge for his father's death.

His symbols are a falcon-headed man, a falcon, a lion with the head of a falcon, a sphinx and a falcon resting on the neck of the pharaoh, spreading his wings to either side of the pharaoh's head and whispering guidance in his ear.

Geb

Geb is the god of the Earth. Geb is shown as a man who wears either a white crown or a goose. The goose was his sacred animal. He is seen lying on his side. Earthquakes were thought of as the laughter of Geb.

As time went by, the pharaoh and the priests felt it was important to have a god that looked after the common people. This was Isis.

Although some gods were worshipped all over Egypt, each part of Egypt also had its own gods. For example, the main god of Thebes was Amun.

A land of rituals

The pharaoh was a god to the people of ancient Egypt and the main representative of the people to the gods in heaven. The pharaoh, as the link between the gods and the people, was a living god.

Osiris

Osiris was the god of the underworld. He is shown as a mummified pharaoh, seated, and holding in his hands the sceptre and the flail or whip (symbols of a king), sometimes with a crown having a pair of ostrich feathers at its base.

Osiris was second only to his father, Re, and was the leader of the gods on Earth. He was the husband of Isis and the father of Horus.

In one of the best known myths of ancient Egypt, Osiris was murdered by his evil brother, Set, and torn into fourteen pieces. His wife, Isis, gathered up all of the pieces and for a while brought Osiris back to life. But Osiris has to remain in the underworld because the dead may not permanently return to the land of the living.

In the underworld, Osiris sits on a great throne, where he is praised by the souls of the just. This part of the underworld is like the land of the living, but without sorrow or pain.

Amun

Amun was worshipped as the creator god of Thebes. Amun was married to Mut and their son was Khonsu, a moon god. Amun was closely connected with the ram. When shown as a king, he wears the crown of two plumes and often sits on a throne.

Eventually Amun (the invisible one) was combined with Re, the Sun, and called Amun-Re. The pharaoh got his power from Amun-Re. In return, the pharaoh supported the temples and the worship of Amun-Re.

Isis

Isis was the mother goddess and represents women. She is shown as a beautiful woman, often wearing a crown which may represent the throne of authority. She sometimes wears the Sun disk, and can also be represented simply as an eye. Isis was the only god worshipped by all Egyptians in all parts of the country. She was prayed to for guidance and peace.

Isis was the daughter of Nut and Geb, the sister and wife to Osiris and the mother of Horus. In the legend of Osiris, it is she who travels the world to find all the pieces of his body and brings him back to life.

The spells and rituals cast by Isis were collected into the BOOK OF THE DEAD.

He was seen as the son of the Sun god, Re, while the dead king was seen as Osiris. So when the kings built pyramids up towards the Sun god Re and the stars, they also built chambers down below the pyramids to show their relationship to Osiris.

Because he was a god, it was vital that the pharaoh's dead body should be preserved forever. This led to the most extraordinary **RITUALS** for burying dead pharaohs (as we see, for example, with Tutankhamun).

Rituals centred around offerings, but there were also many celebrations when, for example, the statue of a god might be carried in public from the sanctuary of their temple so that the common people could see it.

Uniting the gods

Different gods were worshipped in different parts of Egypt for many centuries. Then the pharaohs decided it would be easier to rule if everyone worshipped the same god. They chose Re, the most important god of the north, and combined him with the creator god, Amun of southern Egypt. The new god they called Amun-Re.

The afterlife

The ancient Egyptians believed in an afterlife – that is a place where people went after they died. Some thought of it as a place among the stars, while others thought of it as a place with Osiris in the underworld.

Thoth

Thoth was the Ibis-headed god whose name means 'Truth' and 'Time'. Thoth was a god of creation, but was also thought to be the one who civilised men. It was Thoth who helped Isis work the ritual to bring Osiris back from the dead.

Thoth helped Horus destroy his wicked uncle Set. Thoth was also the representation of Re in the afterlife. He was believed to be the author of the spells in the *Book of the Dead*, he was a helper (and punisher) of the deceased as they tried to enter the underworld.

Anubis

Anubis is thought of as one of the many sons of Osiris. Anubis was the god of EMBALMING and mummification and helped the dead on their path through the underworld.

Anubis is shown as a man with the head of a jackal-like animal. The head is black, showing he is a god of the dead.

Anubis tests the dead on their knowledge of the gods and their faith. He places their heart on the Scales of Justice during the Judging of the Heart, and he feeds the souls of wicked people to Ammit, the crocodile god.

Mummies

To preserve the bodies of the dead, the ancient Egyptians used a process called mummification.

The hot, dry, salty desert sand has a curious effect on buried bodies: it dries them out without letting them rot away. This is called mummification. For many centuries, this happened naturally when bodies were buried in the sand of the Egyptian desert.

Changing ideas

The ancient Egyptians gradually came to believe that part of a person's spirit remained with their dead body. As a result, it became vital to preserve the body, and they worried that bodies simply buried in the sand might be dug up and eaten by wild animals. As a result, they began to bury bodies in wooden coffins.

▼ ① **The stages of mummifying a body.**

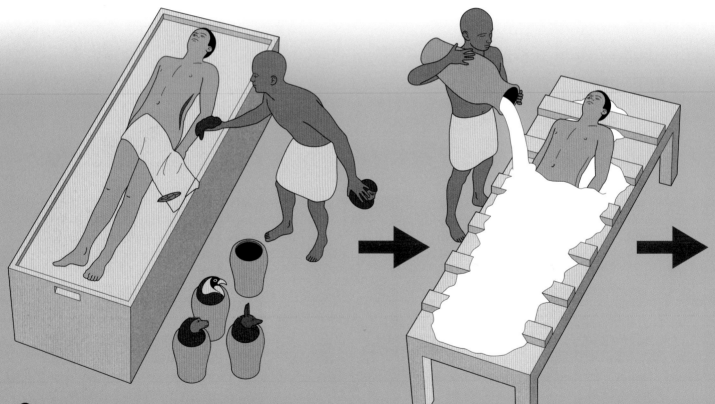

❶ The embalmer first made a cut into the left side of the body with a flint knife, and through this they removed the intestines, liver, lungs and stomach. These were dried out and stored in special vessels called **CANOPIC JARS**. The brains were pulled out through the nose using a long hook, and thrown away. The heart and kidneys were not removed because they were thought to belong with the body.

MAJOR ORGAN	CANOPIC JAR
Lungs	Head of baboon
Stomach	Head of dog
Liver	Head of human
Intestines	Head of falcon

❷ Next, the flesh was thoroughly dried out by packing it inside and out in salts. This drying process took forty days.

However, without being placed in contact with the hot salty sand, the bodies rotted. This meant that when the ancient Egyptians used coffins, they had to find a way to mummify the body before it went in the coffin.

Mummification

Mummification is a combination of **EMBALMING** (preserving the body), saying the correct prayers and going through the correct **RITUALS** (pictures ① and ②). The whole process took seventy days.

◀ ② **A mummified body in a plain wooden coffin. The mummification process was very costly. Only the most wealthy and powerful could afford to be mummified after their death.**

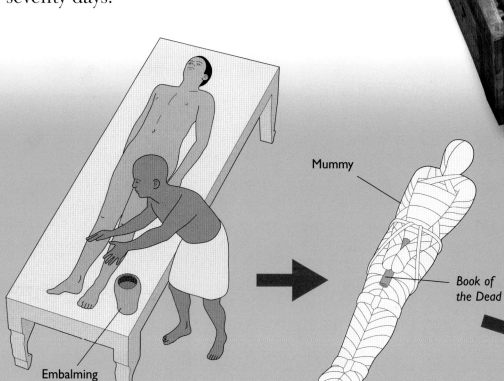

Mummy

Book of the Dead

Embalming oil

❸ Then oils were rubbed into the dried flesh to keep the skin supple. After this the body was packed with sawdust and linen so that it would keep its shape.

❹ The body was next wrapped in strips of linen. The embalmer began by wrapping the fingers and toes, then the head and then the rest of the body.

Lucky charms called **AMULETS** were placed among the wrappings. Each layer of bandage was covered with **RESIN**, a kind of natural glue.

The arms and legs were tied together. A papyrus scroll with spells from their sacred *Book of the Dead* was placed between the wrapped hands.

❺ A cloth was wrapped around the entire body and a picture of the god Osiris was painted on its surface. A final wrapping was added and a painted board placed on the mummy before it was put in the first wooden coffin.

Body-shaped coffin

Coffins

The first coffin was placed in a larger second coffin (picture ⑤).

These coffins were then placed in a final large stone coffin, called a sarcophagus (pictures ③ and ④). The sarcophagus, together with goods that the person would need in the afterlife, were then sealed in the tomb.

Once the tomb was sealed, people could no longer get to the body to pray for it, so a painting remembering the dead person was placed on the outside. Of course, in the case of a pharaoh the tomb was much grander – sometimes even taking the shape of a pyramid – and a temple of remembrance was built somewhere close to the tomb.

▲ ④ Stone sarcophagus.

▼ ③ The stone sarcophagus and gold inner coffin of Tutankhamun in the burial chamber of his tomb.

▶ ⑤ Typical painted wooden, body-shaped coffins from about 1100 BC.

Pyramids

The pyramids are the grandest and most puzzling monuments ever built by the ancient Egyptians. They connected the pharaohs with the Sun and the stars.

Pyramid building belongs only to a part of ancient Egyptian history. For a few generations, pharaohs had gigantic tombs created, and in doing so they built the world's greatest monuments (picture ①). But then pyramid building suddenly stopped.

There are about 108 pyramids in ancient Egypt. All are in the desert overlooking the River Nile. The most famous pyramids are at Giza, on the opposite bank of the River Nile to Cairo. However, pyramid building did not start at Giza, but to the south at a place called Saqqara.

The first pyramids

The earliest pharaohs were buried in chambers cut down into the rock. These chambers were then covered with mounds of soil, and flat-roofed rooms were built on top to hold their grave goods. These buildings are called **MASTABAS**.

Then, about 4,600 years ago, an architect called Imhotep designed a new kind of tomb. He replaced the mastaba with a pyramid.

▲ ① The inside of a pyramid, showing the places where burial chambers have been found. Some were deep underground, while others were inside the pyramid. Tiny tunnels connected them to the outside. There would originally have been a temple next to the entrance tunnel.

The first pyramid he built was for king Djoser. It is now called the Step Pyramid because the steps that it is made of can be seen (pictures ② and ③).

The pyramid was surrounded with a wall to create a private courtyard. The Great Pyramids (see pages 38–39) once had walled courtyards like this, too.

The Bent Pyramid

The ancient Egyptians began to try to improve on the Step Pyramid by building a pyramid with smooth sides.

◀ ② This is how a pyramid might have been built using ramps. When it was built, the ramps were removed.

▼ ③ The Step Pyramid. It is 62 m high and about 113 m along the base.

The first attempt at this is close to the Step Pyramid. It was much steeper than the Step Pyramid. Too steep, in fact. So before it was finished the architects had to redesign the top at a gentler angle. This is why it is called the Bent Pyramid (picture ④).

This pyramid was faced in stone blocks so that the steps could not be seen. The last stage in making a true pyramid had been completed.

▲ ④ The Bent Pyramid.

The pyramids at Giza

The three Great Pyramids at Giza – those of pharaohs Khufu, Khafre and Menkaure – are counted among the Seven Wonders of the Ancient World. They are made of limestone blocks cut from the rock on which they stand, and they are all the work of three pharaohs who lived in a single century 4,500 years ago.

▼ The Sphinx is half human, half lion. The face, 22 times life size, is probably of pharaoh Khafre. The Sphinx is 21 m high and 73 m long. You can see the layers of rock from which it was cut.

These people and horses show the huge size of this **SPHINX**. There are many sphinxes even though we call this one the Sphinx.

This was the tomb of Menkaure. It is 65 m tall. This pyramid is built over a burial chamber cut into the rock below.

This is the pyramid of Khafre. It is just over 136 m high with a base 210 m long. A small amount of its original limestone facing blocks remain near the top. This pyramid covers a burial chamber cut into the rock below.

The Sphinx.

PHARAOHS, GODS, MUMMIES AND LIFE AFTER DEATH

The Great Pyramids were originally faced with white limestone so that they would have glinted in the sunshine. The Khafre pyramid still has a little of this facing stone at the top. All of the rest was removed in later centuries.

The shape of the pyramids relates to a symbol for the Sun god. But the plan of the group of pyramids mirrors the three stars of Orion's Belt in the night sky. They were probably built as an image of heaven on Earth.

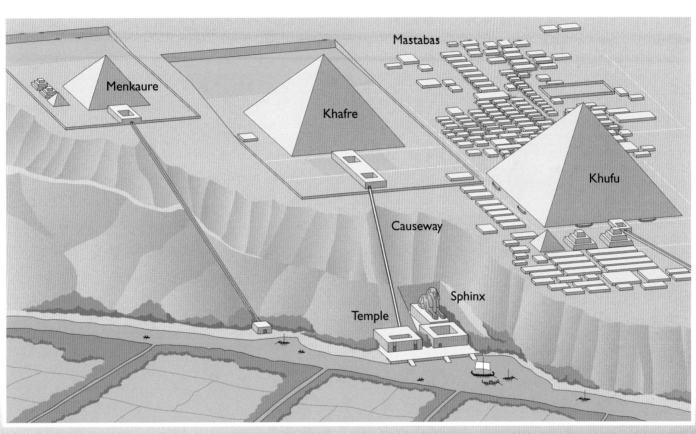

Menkaure

Khafre

Mastabas

Khufu

Causeway

Sphinx

Temple

Built for pharaoh Khufu, this is the oldest and largest pyramid. It is 146 m high and the base of each side is 233 m. Two million blocks of limestone, 20 years and the labours of 20,000 men were needed to build it. This pyramid has a false burial chamber cut into the rock, but the main chambers are within the pyramid. These chambers are connected to the outside by tiny shafts. The shafts point towards the stars.

▲ This is what the pyramids looked like in ancient times. The pharaoh's body would have been brought by boat to the harbour then carried up the steep causeway road to the pyramid.

What were temples like?

Of all the things that remain of ancient Egypt, the temples are among the most striking, even though they lie in ruins.

▼ ② The outer court with its pillars. The roof they supported has gone.

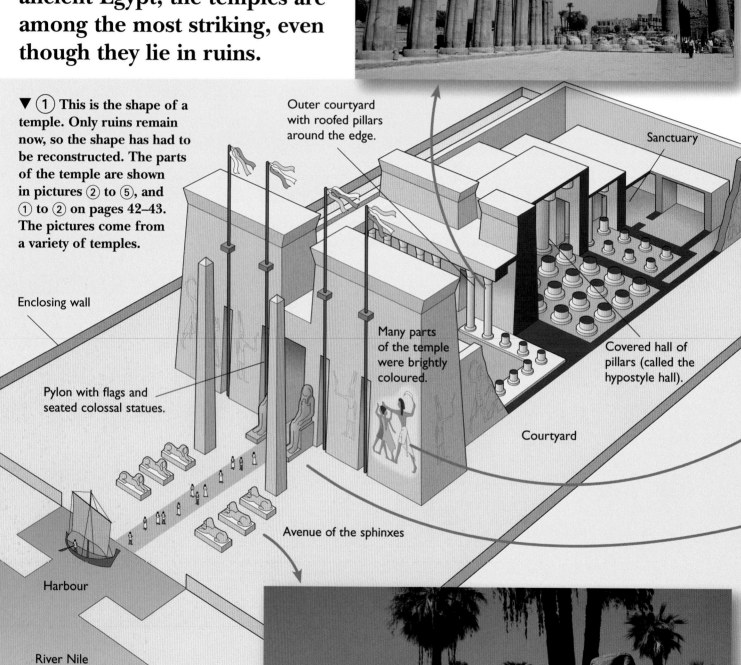

▼ ① This is the shape of a temple. Only ruins remain now, so the shape has had to be reconstructed. The parts of the temple are shown in pictures ② to ⑤, and ① to ② on pages 42–43. The pictures come from a variety of temples.

Outer courtyard with roofed pillars around the edge.

Sanctuary

Enclosing wall

Pylon with flags and seated colossal statues.

Many parts of the temple were brightly coloured.

Covered hall of pillars (called the hypostyle hall).

Courtyard

Avenue of the sphinxes

Harbour

River Nile

▶ ③ Part of the avenue of the sphinxes that connect the temples at Luxor and Karnak.

Weblink: www.CurriculumVisions.com

The ancient Egyptians were great builders. Their most complicated buildings were the temples built to honour the gods. Today they mostly lie in ruins because, centuries ago, conquering peoples deliberately destroyed the temples and stole many of the stones to make new buildings.

▼ ④ Carvings on the outer walls tell of the pharaoh's successful battles and also show the gods. This shows Cleopatra (left) with her son Caesarion making offerings to the god Hathor.

Temples of Thebes

Of all the remains of temples, those near modern day Luxor in Upper Egypt are the most impressive (pictures ① to ⑤). This was the site of the ancient Egyptian capital named Waset which we now call Thebes. The temples were arranged to face the Nile.

Thebes was chosen as a capital city because it was far from the northern borders (where battles were common) and close to the source of Egyptian gold in the desert to the south.

▼ ⑤ The entrance wall, or PYLON, of the Luxor temple. Notice the seated colossal statues (of Ramesses II) and the OBELISK (there used to be two) originally built by Hatshepsut.

The pharaoh's grand procession

After arriving in the temple harbour, the pharaoh's journey to the sanctuary was spectacular.

Imagine the scene as the pharaoh arrives at the temple harbour on his royal boat.

He is carried on a stone-surfaced road lined by **SPHINXES**, statues that are half animal, half man. The ordinary people look on in awe at the face of the pharaoh as he is carried past them.

The temple entrance

Now the pharaoh approaches the main entrance wall, or **PYLON**, which guards the entrance to the temple. It is an immense, wedge-shaped wall which slopes back from a wide base to a narrower top. In the middle is a huge gate. Flags fly from the pylon. On either side of the gateway are immense seated statues and towering **OBELISKS**.

The procession continues through the gate and into a courtyard edged with many pillars. Here, waiting for him, are the priests and other important people.

The pharaoh crosses the courtyard and enters a hall almost filled with pillars (picture ①). Each pillar is finely carved with hieroglyphs telling stories of the pharaohs and the gods. The pharaoh looks up at the ceiling and sees it covered in paintings of heavenly boats and stars.

Now accompanied only by the high priests, he moves on to a small room with statues of the gods. It is called the **SANCTUARY** (picture ②). This is the most sacred part of the temple.

The pharaoh now prepares to meet with the gods, to speak to them and receive their messages.

▼ ② This small, dark room is the sanctuary of the temple.

◀ ① The spectacular pillared hall (hypostyle hall).

Famous pharaohs in history

There were about 30 dynasties (royal lines) and hundreds of pharaohs during the long period of ancient Egyptian civilisation. Most of the famous pharaohs belong to either the early part of the Old Kingdom or to the New Kingdom, and in particular to the 18th and 19th dynasties.

DJOSER (2687–2668 BC), 3rd dynasty
Djoser was the founder of the 3rd dynasty and one of the greatest of the early pharaohs. His chief architect, Imhotep, was responsible for building the first pyramid (the Step Pyramid).

SNEFRU (2613–2589 BC), 4th dynasty
Snefru was the first ruler of the 4th dynasty and the pharaoh who began to unite Egypt. He was responsible for the Bent Pyramid.

KHUFU (2589–2566 BC), 4th dynasty
Khufu (also known as Cheops) was the son of Snefru and the builder of the Great Pyramid at Giza.

KHAFRE (2558–2532 BC), 4th dynasty
Khafre was a son of Khufu and the builder of the second largest pyramid at Giza. Khafre built his pyramid on higher ground, giving the illusion that his pyramid was taller than the pyramid of Khufu.

MENKAURE (2532–2503 BC), 4th dynasty
Menkaure was a son of Khafre and the builder of the third pyramid at Giza. Much smaller than the other two pyramids, it had to be completed by his son.

HATSHEPSUT (1479–1458 BC), 18th dynasty
Hatshepsut was the daughter of Thutmose I and Queen Ahmose. She married her half-brother, Thutmose II, who had a son, Thutmose III, by another of his wives. When Thutmose II died in 1479 BC, his son, Thutmose III, was too young to become pharaoh and Hatshepsut was appointed to rule jointly. However, in 1473 she decided that she would rule alone.

Because pharaohs were supposed to be men, Hatshepsut dressed like a man when holding court, but she still wore perfume and make-up like a woman.

Hatshepsut was responsible for building the obelisks in the temples, a design that had never been used before. She also built a magnificent temple near the Valley of the Kings (picture ①).

We do not know what happened to Hatshepsut after 1458 BC because she suddenly disappears from the records and Thutmose III takes over as pharaoh.

▼▶ ① The MORTUARY TEMPLE and statues of Hatshepsut.

THUTMOSE III (1458–1425 BC) (Another spelling is Thutmosis), 18th dynasty

Because Hatshepsut was so powerful, Thutmose had to keep a low profile for many years. Thutmose may have led a revolt against Hatshepsut or she may simply have died, we do not know. But we do know he eventually became ruler. Thutmose III has been called the Napoleon of ancient Egypt because he fought and won many battles. He had them recorded in great detail on temple walls. His most famous battle was winning at Megiddo after a long siege. At the end he took 894 chariots, 200 suites of armour, 2,000 horses, 25,000 other animals and a large number of slaves. He claimed to have captured 350 cities.

The most important god to Thutmose was Amun, the god of Karnak temple. At this time the temple had many additions because the wealth of the spoils taken in battle were partly spent on the temple.

Thutmose had Hatshepsut's name removed from monuments, but as he did not do this for many years, he might have been encouraged to do it for political reasons, not hatred of his stepmother. But the obelisks she had built were sacred monuments and he could not have them defaced. So, instead, he had brick walls built around them. This is why they survive.

AKHENATEN (ruled 1352–1336 BC), 18th dynasty

Akhenaten was first named Amenhotep IV (picture ②). His chief wife was the famous and beautiful Nefertiti. But Nefertiti did not bear him a son. His son, Tutankhaten, who later renamed himself Tutankhamun, was by another wife.

▶ ② One of the few surviving statues of Akhenaten.

Amenhotep IV became convinced that the worship of the ancient gods, headed by Amun-Re, was wrong, and that there was only one true god, the Sun god, Aten. So he changed his name to Akhenaten (meaning 'Servant of the Aten') and then caused enormous disruption to the Egyptians by closing all of the temples dedicated to Amun. He also decided to move his capital 300 km north of Thebes and build a new city in the desert (now called Amarna).

Akhenaten declared that the Sun god stretched down directly to him, and so no priests were needed. Clearly, this angered the priests, who were now without a source of wealth and power. They bided their time.

Akhenaten sent his officials to destroy the temples of Amun. With Akhenaten taking less interest in affairs of state, it was his general, Horemheb, who was left to keep everything under control.

Nefertiti died in the 12th year of Akhenaten's reign and Akhenaten died in 1336 BC, after reigning for 16 years.

◀ ③ **A colossal statue of Ramesses II at Karnak.**

TUTANKHAMUN (1334–1325 BC), 18th dynasty

When Akhenaten died, Smenkhkare (smen-car-ee) ruled for a short while (1338–1336), then died and the throne passed to his brother Tutankhaten. Tutankhaten gave up the new religion of his father (probably because of strong pressure from powerful priests) and changed his name to Tutankhamun, or 'living image of the god Amun'.

Tutankhamun died when he was about 17, probably from an infection after breaking a leg either in sport or in battle. Because he died young, Tutankhamun played a minor role in Egyptian history. He concentrated on rebuilding the temples at Thebes that his father had destroyed. But his was the only grave to be discovered unlooted and so his is the only example we have of the fabulous wealth buried with the pharaohs (see pages 14–17).

Even Tutankhamun's famous tomb is a mystery because it is very small. This is why it was missed by grave robbers and why it was left untouched until Howard Carter found it in 1922.

The tomb is so crowded that it seems as though he was buried in a hurry in a tomb meant for someone else, possibly a noble. But we have no idea why this was.

HOREMHEB (1323–1295 BC), 18th dynasty

Horemheb was the last ruler of the 18th dynasty. He was Tutankhamun's army commander. He took over when Tutankhamun died without a son.

RAMESSES II (1279–1213 BC), (also spelled Rameses, Ramesses known as Ramesses the Great), 19th dynasty

Ramesses II was the son of pharaoh Seti I. Ramesses was extraordinarily long-lived, had 200 wives, 96 sons and 60 daughters. He survived at least 13 of his sons.

Ramesses II ruled for 66 years. In his long life he is famous for having colossal statues made of himself (picture ③).

He lived from about 1302 BC to 1213 BC and reigned from 1279 BC. In 1274 BC Ramesses defeated the Hittites at the battle of Kadesh. He had his victory sculpted on many temple walls. Ramesses started many building projects, but the most famous is the southern temple at Abu Simbel, on the border with Nubia.

Glossary

AMULET A charm, made of precious stone and shaped to represent gods or sacred animals. Amulets were worn as jewellery during life, and were placed within the mummy wrappings as good luck charms for the afterlife.

ARCHAEOLOGIST A person who investigates civilisations from the remains they leave behind (rather than from written records).

BOOK OF THE DEAD The ancient Egyptian sacred book of spells and hymns.

CANOPIC JARS A set of four, god-headed jars used to store a dead person's embalmed organs. The organs were protected by the four sons of Horus: Duamutef (stomach), Qebhsenuef (intestines), Hapi (lungs), and Imsety (liver).

CARTOUCHE An oval with a straight line set against it, and which contains the hieroglyphs of a pharaoh.

CATARACT A large waterfall or rapid. The First and Second Cataracts of the Nile made important boundaries in ancient Egypt.

CIVILISATION A group of people who live in a well developed, town-based society that follows legal and religious rules. The term comes from the Latin *civis*, meaning "citizen" or "townsman."

DELTA The triangle of flat land created by a river as it enters the sea.

DIVINE Something that comes from a god.

DYNASTY A group of related royal rulers.

EMBALM To treat a dead body with chemicals in order to preserve it.

GRAVE GOODS Anything found in the same place as a burial are called grave goods. This is where we find most objects from ancient Egypt.

HIEROGLYPHS, HIEROGLYPHICS The system of picture writing is called hieroglyphics, the individual pictures are hieroglyphs and are similar to the letters of an alphabet.

HITTITES An ancient people based in what is now modern Turkey.

LOWER EGYPT The part of ancient Egypt near the Nile delta.

MASTABA A flat-roofed room over a burial chamber. It was designed to hold the goods the dead person would need in the afterlife.

MORTUARY TEMPLE A temple of remembrance to a dead person. The mortuary temples of some pharaohs were immense buildings.

MUMMY, MUMMIFICATION The process of preserving the body is called mummification. The preserved body is called a mummy.

OBELISK A tall square based pyramid with a pointed top carved as a symbol of the Sun god, Re. Obelisks were placed in pairs in front of the temple pylon.

PAPYRUS A kind of paper made of crushed rushes.

PHARAOH A king of ancient Egypt. Pharaohs were supposed to be men, but there were woman pharaohs, too. Hatshepsut and Cleopatra are the most famous.

PYLON The massive sloping wall at the front of the temple.

PYRAMID A four-sided triangular tomb designed to be a symbol of the Sun god, Re.

RESIN A natural plastic that hardens when exposed to the air.

RITUAL A ceremony having precisely defined rules.

SANCTUARY A place of safety. The heart of a temple where the gods might come down to Earth.

SARCOPHAGUS A stone coffin.

SOLAR BOAT A boat built to carry the pharaoh to heaven after he died. It was built in the shape of a Nile rowing boat.

SPHINX A creature made of two different kinds of animal. The body was usually that of a lion, the head that of a man. But the head could also be a ram.

TEMPLE A general name for a place of worship.

UPPER EGYPT The part of ancient Egypt based on Thebes.

Weblink: www.CurriculumVisions.com

Index